To:
_____

From:
_____

This book is dedicated to every niece, nephew, godchild and all the children who have touched my life, especially my beautiful niece, Briana, and wonderful nephew, Alixander who inspired me to write this book at the time of their innocence. —Geralda Aldajuste

©2021 Geralda Aladjuste. All Rights Reserved.
No part of this book may be reproduced, stored in a retrieval system, or transmitted by any means without the written permission of the author.

ISBN: 978-1-7367483-1-2 (paperback)
ISBN: 978-1-7367483-3-6 (ebook)
Library of Congress Cataloging-in-Publication Data
Library of Congress Control Number: 2021915320

Published by Vine Publishing, Inc. (New York, NY - www.vinepublish.com)
Printed in the United States of America

GERALDA ALDAJUSTE

Knowing God From A-Z

Illustrated by: Girlvsworld

 is for **amazing** — Lord, no other gods compare to you. (Psalm 40:5)

 is for **awesome** — You are great! You keep your promises to everyone. (Psalm 118:23)

B is for **beautiful** — Your glory shines like the sun. (Psalm 50:2)

b is for **blameless** — You can always be trusted; you never do wrong. (Deuteronomy 32:3-4)

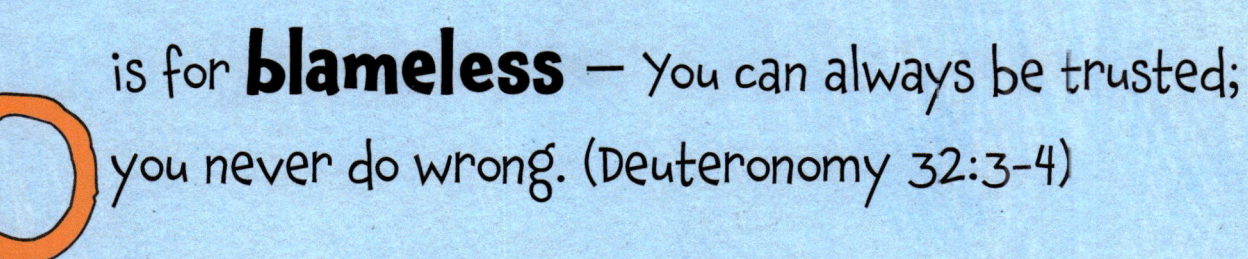

C is for **caring** — You take care of us. (Psalm 23:1-3)

C is for **Creator** — You created everything. You created heaven and earth. You created what we see and what we do not see. (Colossians 1:16)

D is for **defender** — You are on our side. You take up for us when others come against us. (Proverbs 23:11)

 is for **dependable** — You do not tell lies or change your mind. God, you always keep your promises. (Numbers 23:19)

E is for **eternal** – Lord, you are the Alpha (beginning) and Omega (End), the first and the last. (Revelation 22:13)

e is for **encourager** — Lord, you told us not to worry about anything but pray about everything. (Philippians 4:6)

F is for **Father** — Lord, you are my heavenly Father. You take care of me. (1 John 3:1)

f is for **friend** — Lord, you are my true friend.
(John 15:15)

G is for **great** – Lord, you are stronger and greater than anyone or anything. I know that things can happen when I call your name. (Jeremiah 10:6)

g is for **good** – Lord, you are always good. You will always love me and you are always there for me. (Psalm 100:5)

h is for **honest** — Lord, I believe you because you do not lie. (Titus 1:2)

I is for **incredible** — I thank you that sometimes you will do more and give me more than I asked you for. Your imagination is bigger than mine. (Ephesians 3:20)

I is for **invisible** — No one has ever seen God.
(John 1:18)

J is for **judge** – God, you know everything I do and you help me to know whether it is good or bad. (Ecclesiastes 12:14)

j is for **joy** — Lord, I can come to you when I am feeling sad, and you will give me joy. (Psalm 30:5)

K is for **kind** – Lord, thank you for not being angry with me, and showing me love.
(Psalm 103:8)

L is for **love** — Lord, you love me no matter what. (1 John 4:19)

L is for **life** — God, thank you giving me my family and everyone I know life.
(Genesis 2:7)

M is for **mighty** — Lord, you are stronger than everyone in the world. (Job 9:4)

N is for **nature** — God, you created the trees, animals, my friends and family. You created everything!
(John 1:3)

N is for **near** — Lord, no matter where I am, You are near. I don't have to be fearful because you are always with me. (Deuteronomy 31:6)

O is for **omnipresent**— Lord, you are everywhere and there is nothing hidden from your sight. (Proverbs 15:3)

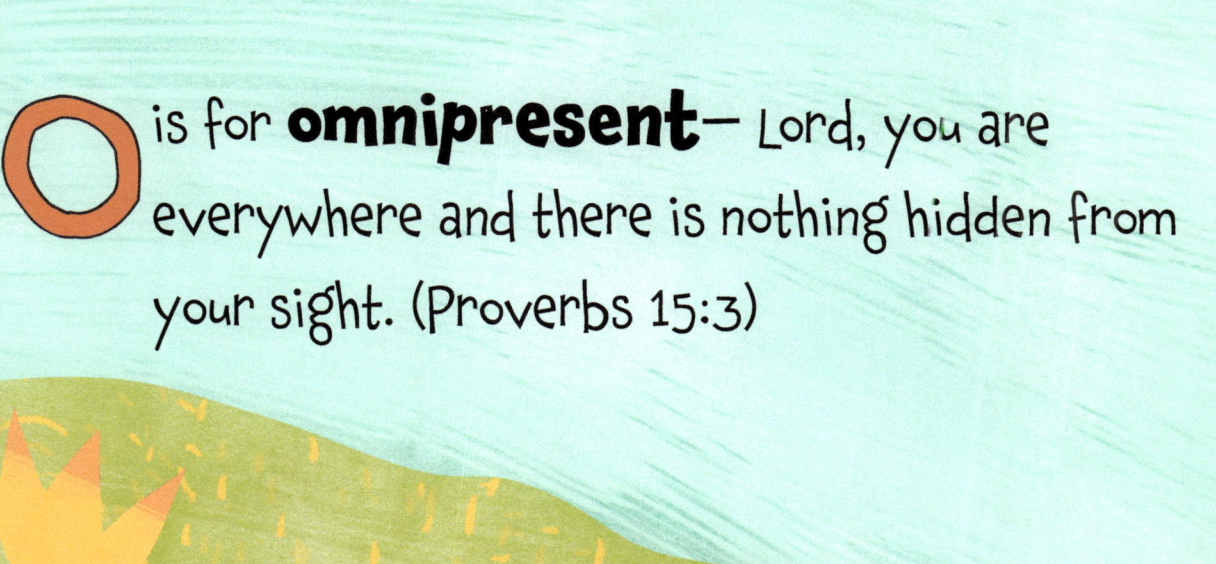

p is for **patient** – Lord, you help me to kind and patient. (1 Corinthians 13:4)

Q is for **quiet** — Lord you help me to understand that there is a time to be silent, a time to speak. (Ecclesiastes 3:7)

q is for **quench** — Jesus, thank you for quenching my thirst. (John 7:37-38)

r is for **reliable** – God, thank you for always helping me. (Psalm 54:4)

R is for **rescuer** — Father, thank you for sending your son, Jesus to rescue me. (John 3:16-17)

S is for **shield** — God, you are my help and my shield. (Psalm 33.20)

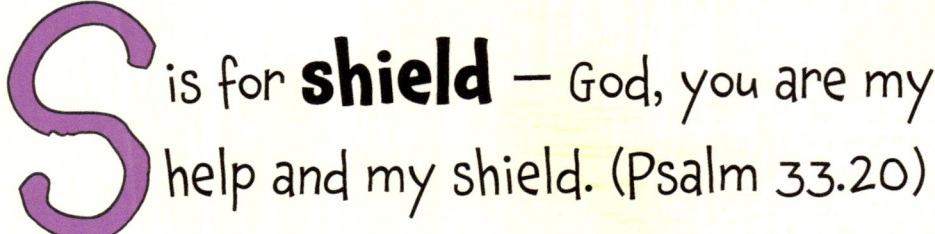

S is for **Spirit** — God you are Spirit and I must worship you in spirit and in truth. (John 4:24)

T is for **truth** – Goo[d] the truth, so that the[...] free. (John 8:32)

rant us to know
will make us

t is for **trusted** — God, I am happy when I trust in you. (Jeremiah 17:7)

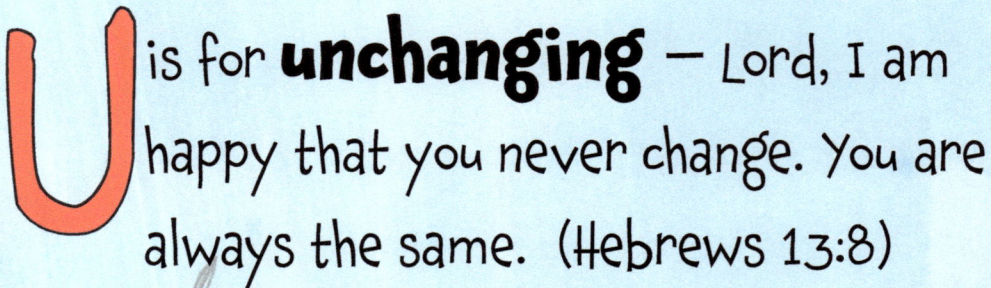

U is for **unchanging** — Lord, I am happy that you never change. You are always the same. (Hebrews 13:8)

U is for **unfailing** — God, you never fail. Your promises are sure.
(2 Corinthians 1:20)

V is for **victorious** — No matter what happens, God has given me victory.
(Romans 8:37)

V is for **vine** — Lord, because I stay close to you, I can do and be who you want me to be. (John 15:5)

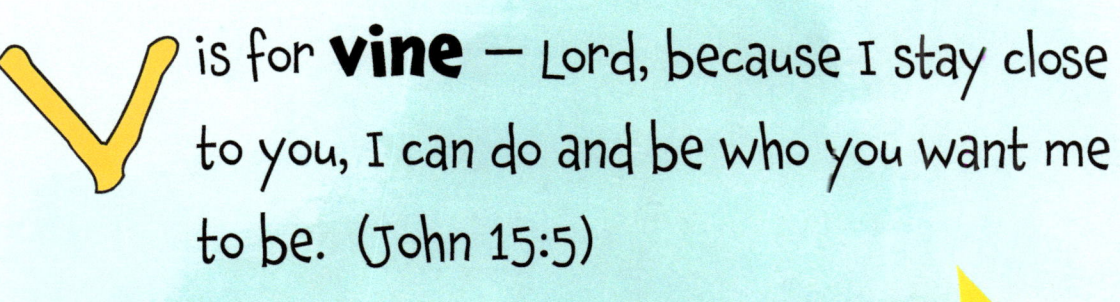

W is for **wisdom** – Lord, no one is smarter than you, and you help me to make wise decisions.". (Proverbs 2:6)

X is for **eXcellent** — God your name is excellent. You are above everything. (Psalm 8:1)

Y is for **yahweh** — God, you are the true and living God. You remain faithful to your people. (Exodus 15:3)

God Loves You!

Geralda Aldajuste

Rev. Geralda Aldajuste loves children and believes in the importance of social justice, as such, she serves on the board of directors for Haiti Hope House, a non-profit organization inspired by Rev. Franck Aguilh. Haiti Hope House operates in Mizak, Haiti, and seeks opportunities to educate, equip and provide hope for Haitian children. In addition, Geralda serves on the board of directors for Faith in NJ, a growing multi-faith and multi-racial network of faith leaders and faith communities working together to advance a social and economic justice agenda at the Local, State, and Federal level.

Geralda is not only a professor or a Licensed Funeral Director licensed in both NY & NJ, but she is also a Certified Grief Recovery Specialist, Notary Public, Life Insurance Agent, and the Pastor of St. Paul United Methodist Church in Willingboro, NJ. She is also a former Hospice Volunteer, Clinical Pastoral Education Chaplain (CPE), Medical Death Investigator, and Middlesex County Medical Examiner's Bereavement Counselor. In March of 2019, she completed certification as a Life coach from P4 Coaching Institute.

A leader in her community, Geralda recently joined the NAACP Willingboro Chapter, the NAACP Delaware Valley Chapter, and the Continentals Societies, Inc, the South Jersey Chapter, an organization that fosters, promotes, and develops the welfare of underprivileged children and youth.